D1742431

James Rae

Zoo Time!

12 Easy Zoological Pieces

12 tierisch leichte Stücke

for alto saxophone and piano

für Altsaxophon und Klavier

Preface

This collection of fun-based pieces was inspired by the antics of our good friends at the Zoo. They are all based on well-known dance forms, Jive, Polka, Waltz etc., and portray, with a little imagination, how creatures other than human beings would perform on the dance floor!

As with *Child's Play* (UE 21 699), the pieces are all in a comfortable range but contain more challenging rhythms and articulations. The piano accompaniments are stylistically supportive and teacher-friendly. They also include chord symbols for improvisation purposes.

James Rae, June 2019

Vorwort

Diese Sammlung von Stücken mit lustigem Charakter wurde von den Abenteuern unserer tierischen Freunde im Zoo inspiriert. Die Grundlage bilden dabei beliebte Tänze wie Jive, Polka oder Walzer. Mit ein wenig Fantasie kann man heraushören, wie sich die Tiere beim Tanzen vergnügen!

Alle Stücke sind genauso wie bei *Child's Play* (UE 21 699) in angenehmer Lage geschrieben, allerdings ist die Rhythmik und Artikulation etwas anspruchsvoller. Die Klavierbegleitung unterstützt die jungen Spielerinnen und Spieler, kommt den Lehrern dabei aber auch entgegen. Für Improvisierfreudige sind zudem Akkordsymbole enthalten.

James Rae, Juni 2019

Préface

Ce recueil de pièces amusantes a été inspiré par les facéties de nos amis du zoo. Elles suivent toutes le format de danses connues (jive, polka, valse, etc.), et décrivent, avec un peu d'imagination, comment nos amies les bêtes évolueraient sur la piste de danse !

Comme celles de *Child's Play* (UE 21 699), ces pièces restent toutes dans un registre confortable, mais elles contiennent des rythmes et des articulations plus complexes. Les accompagnements de piano sont typiques de chaque style et pensés pour les professeurs. Pour permettre l'improvisation, les partitions comportent également des symboles d'accords.

James Rae, juin 2019

Inhalt • Contents • Table des matières

Free Downloads • Gratis Downloads • Téléchargements gratuits :
- Illustrations for colouring • Illustrationen zum Anmalen • Illustrations à colorier

⟶ www.universaledition.com/service-ue21738

James Rae: Zoo Time! – Alto Saxophone

Illustrations by Wendy Sinclair
Cover design by Lynette Williamson

UE 21738
ISMN 979-0-008-08840-7
UPC 8-03452-07222-5
ISBN 978-3-7024-7511-6

2

Tiger Tango

James Rae
(* 1957)

Stealthily! ♩ = 100

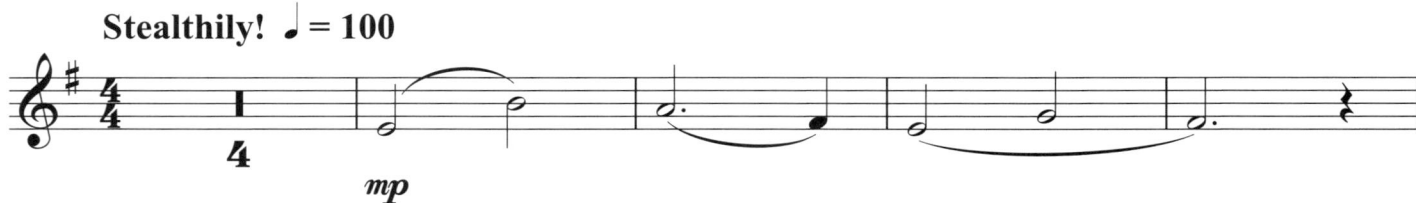

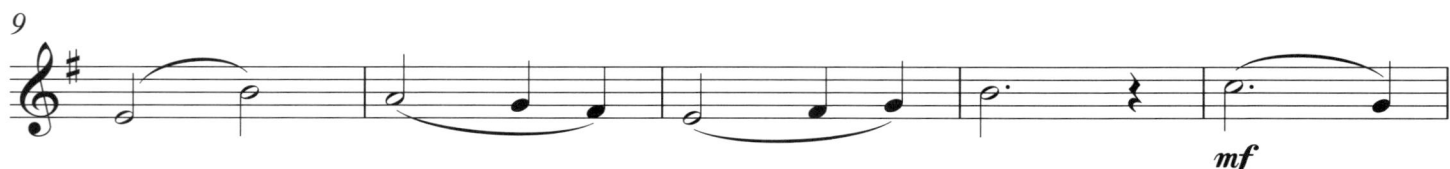

Universal Edition UE 21 738

Rhino Rumba

James Rae

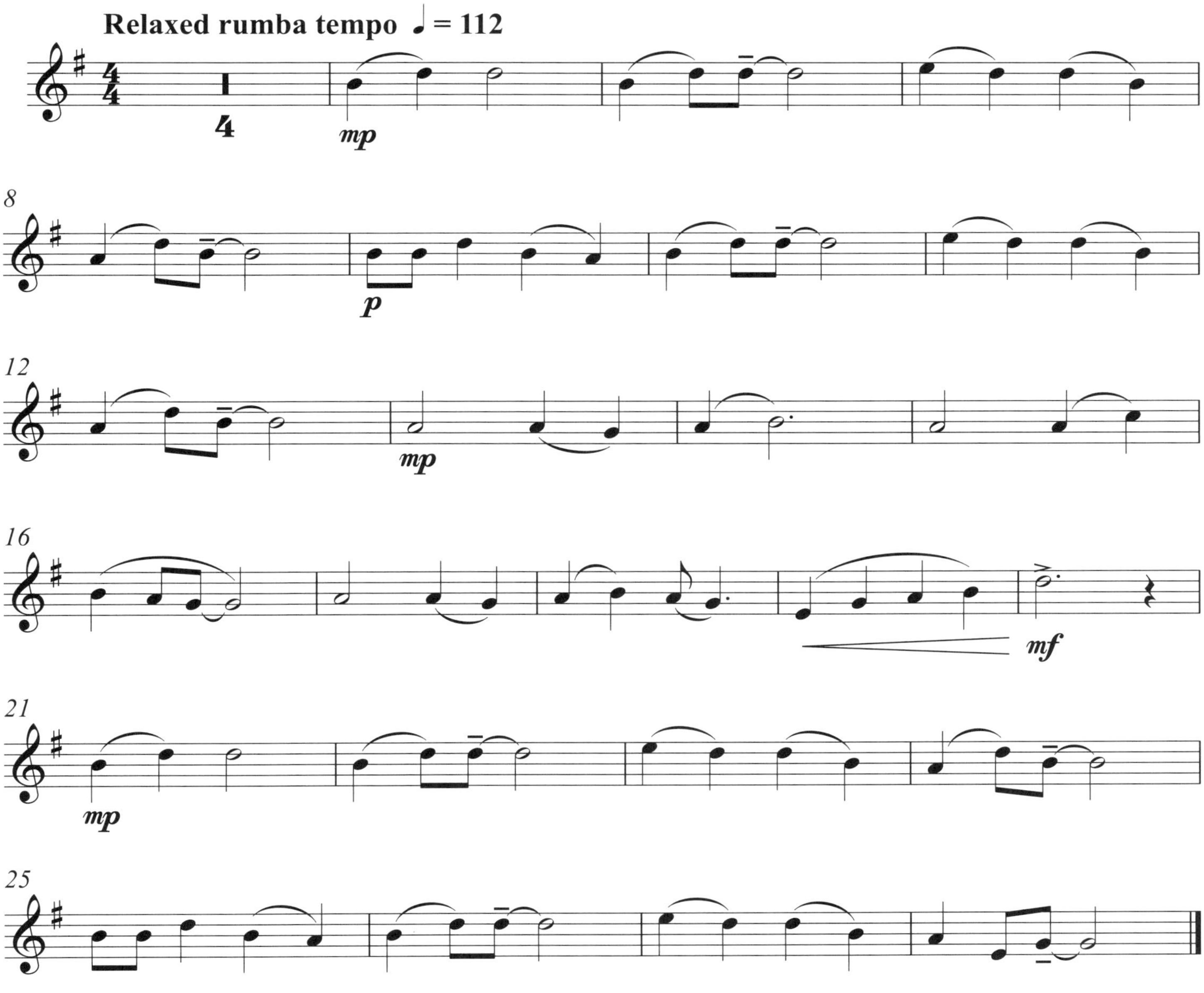

Relaxed rumba tempo ♩ = 112

UE 21 738

4

Toucan Trot

James Rae

Chirpily with humour ♩ = 148

UE 21 738

Polar Bear Boogie

James Rae

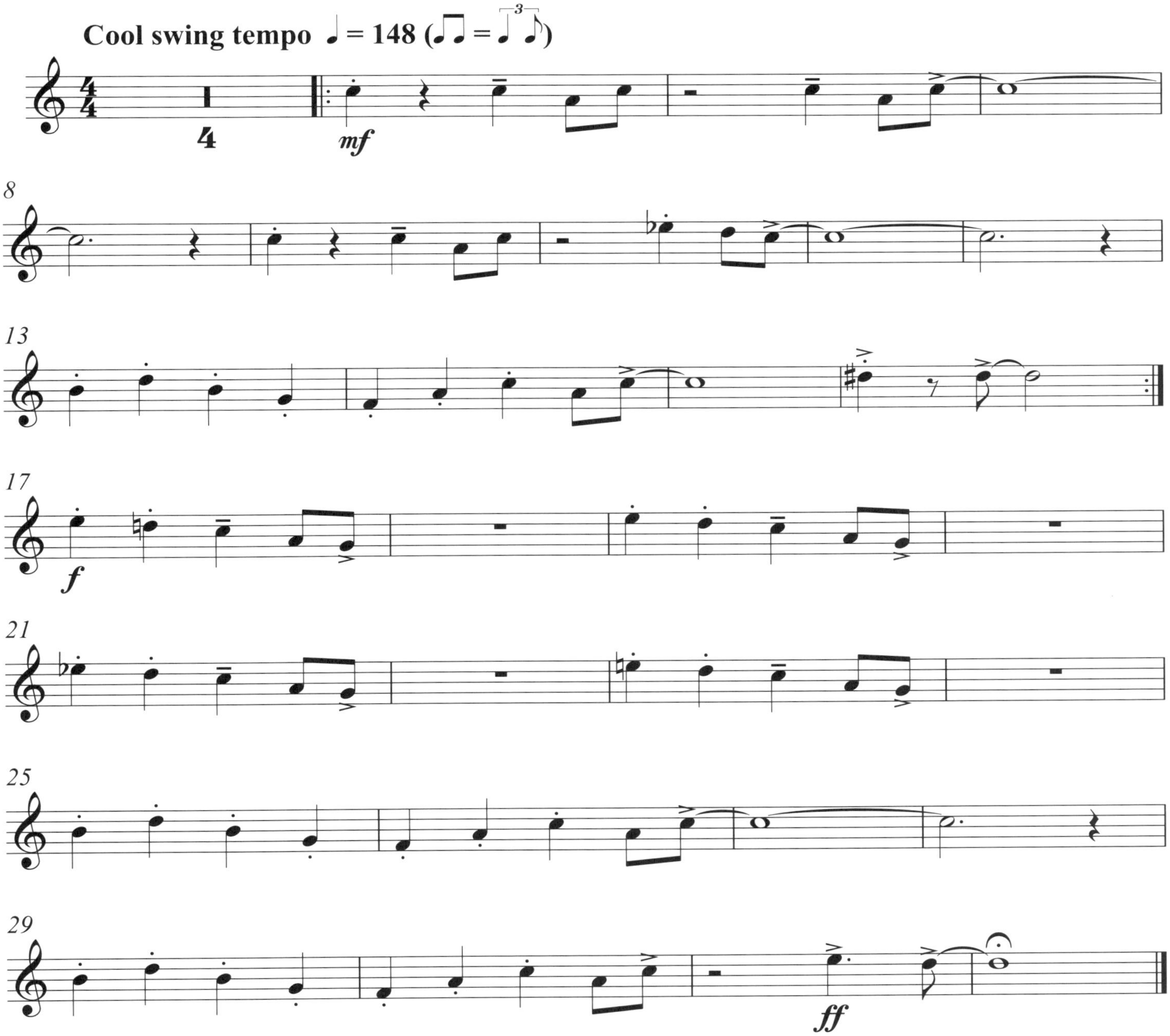

Cool swing tempo ♩ = 148

UE 21 738

Wallaby Waltz

James Rae

Gentle jazz waltz tempo ♩ = 100

UE 21 738

James Rae

Zoo Time!

12 Easy Zoological Pieces
12 tierisch leichte Stücke

for alto saxophone and piano
für Altsaxophon und Klavier

Inhalt · Contents · Table des matières

Tiger Tango

James Rae
(* 1957)

Stealthily! ♩ = 100

Alto Saxophone in E♭

Piano

Gm

Gm   D⁷/G   B♭/G

Am/G   Gm   D⁷/G   B♭/G

G⁷   Cm⁷   F⁷   B♭maj7

Universal Edition UE 21 738 a

Rhino Rhumba

James Rae

UE 21 738 a

Toucan Trot

James Rae

UE 21 738 a

Polar Bear Boogie

James Rae

UE 21 738 a

Wallaby Waltz

James Rae

UE 21 738 a

Penguin Polka

James Rae

UE 21 738 a

Cobra Calypso

James Rae

UE 21 738 a

Lion Lambada

James Rae

UE 21 738 a

Chimpanzee Cha-Cha-Cha

James Rae

UE 21 738 a

Hippo Hop

James Rae

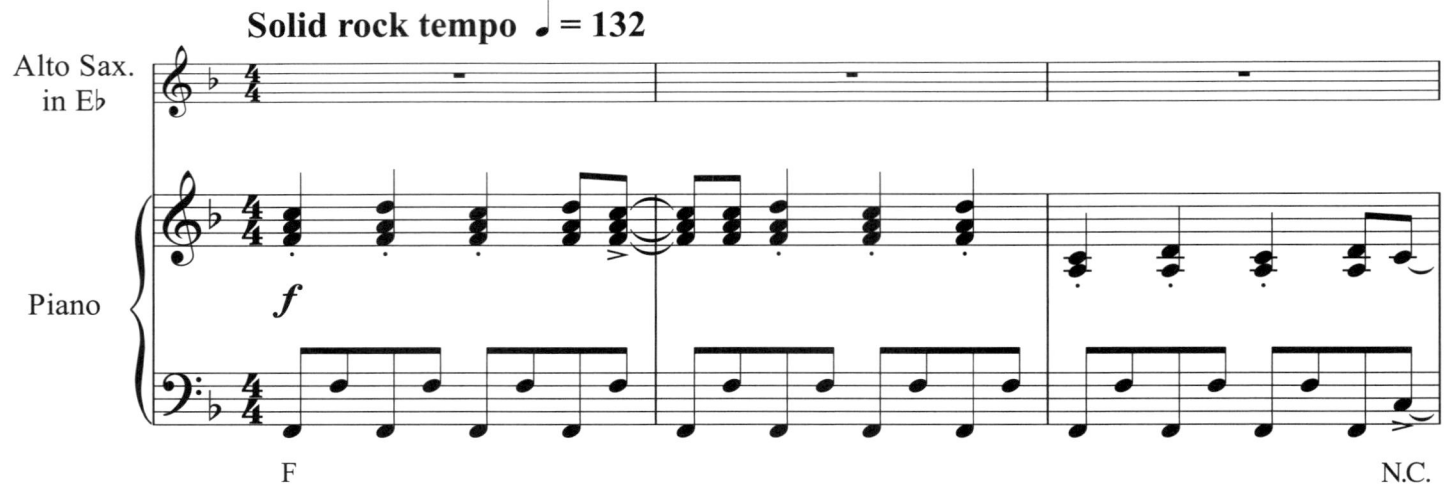

UE 21 738 a

Giraffe Jive

James Rae

UE 21 738 a

Gorilla Gavotte

James Rae

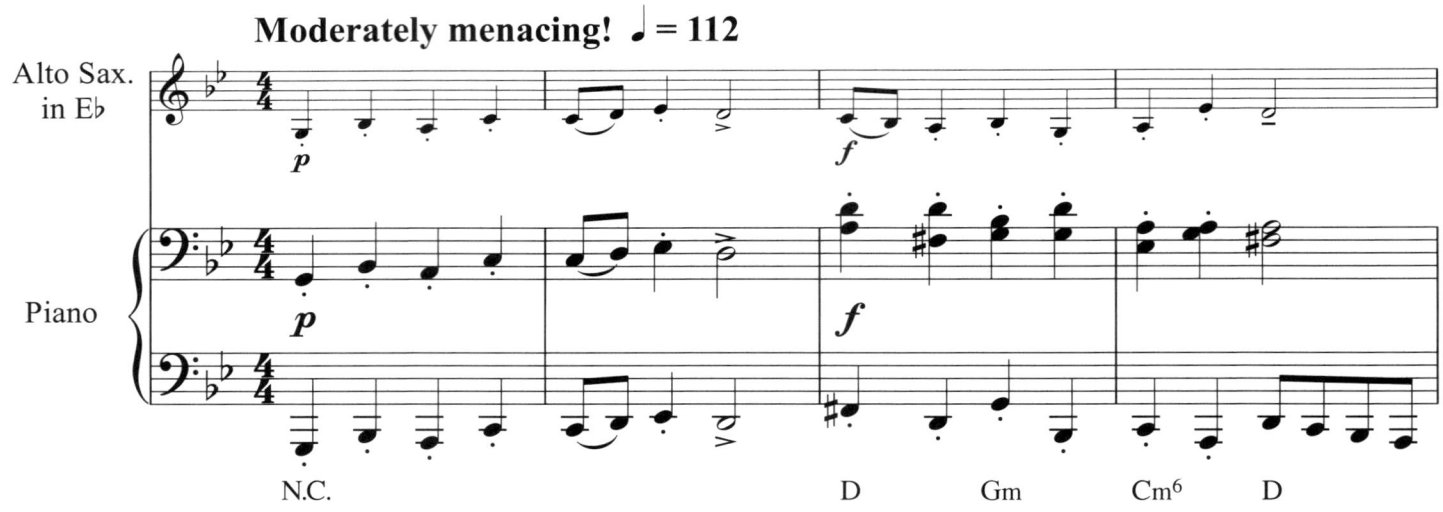

UE 21 738 a

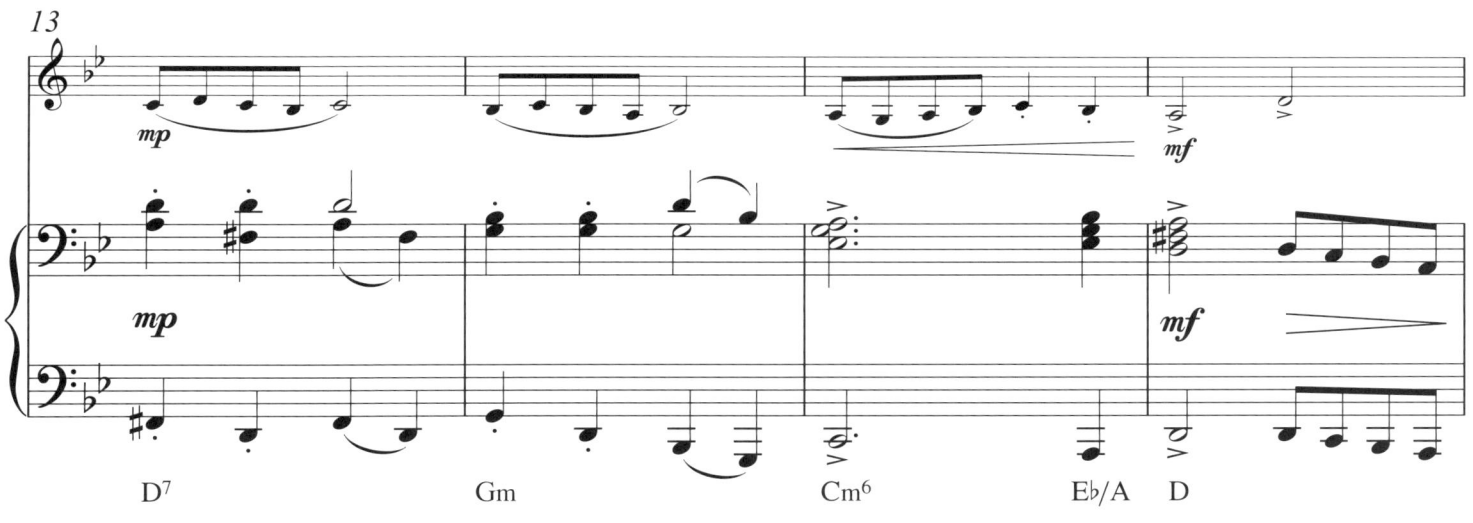

Saxophone Albums and Tutors
in Lighter Styles

■ EASY

James Rae • Introducing the Saxophone Plus Book 1 (alto sax. & pno.) • UE 30420

James Rae • Saxophone Debut (alto sax. + CD) • UE 21530

■ EASY TO INTERMEDIATE

James Rae • Introducing the Saxophone (Engl.) (alto sax. + CD) • UE 17390

James Rae • James Rae's Methode für Saxophon (Germ.) (alto sax. + CD) • UE 31499

James Rae • Introducing the Saxophone Plus Book 2 (alto sax. & pno.) • UE 30421

James Rae • Introducing Saxophone – Duets (2 sax.) • UE 21359

James Rae • Introducing Saxophone – Trios (3 sax. incl. tenor part) • UE 21360

James Rae • Introducing Saxophone – Quartets (4 sax. incl. tenor parts) • UE 21361

Repertoire Explorer Alto Saxophone (alto sax. & pno.) *ed. James Rae* • UE 21486

Repertoire Explorer Tenor Saxophone (tenor sax. & pno.) *ed. James Rae* • UE 21612

The Best of James Rae (alto sax. & pno. or CD) • UE 21408

Blue Baroque Saxophone (alto or tenor sax. & pno.) *arr. James Rae* • UE 21465

James Rae • Jazz Zone (alto or tenor sax. + CD) • UE 21030

James Rae • Sounds Irish (alto or tenor sax. & pno.) • UE 21080

James Rae • 36 More Modern Studies for Solo Saxophone (soprano, alto, tenor or baritone sax.) • UE 21613

■ INTERMEDIATE

Take Ten – Popular Pieces from Bach to Bacharach (alto sax. & pno.) *arr. James Rae* • UE 18836

Take Another Ten (alto or tenor sax. & pno.) *arr. James Rae* • UE 21170

Scott Joplin – 5 Rags (alto or tenor sax. & pno.) *arr. James Rae* • UE19662

Play-Along Saxophone – Blues, Boogie & Ballads (alto or tenor sax. + CD)
arr. Christian Bachner • UE 31854

James Rae • The Tyne Sonata (alto sax. & pno.) • UE 21578

■ WORLD MUSIC PLAY-ALONG (alto or tenor sax. & CD, pno. ad lib.)

Yale Strom • Klezmer • UE 34166

Jovino Santos Neto • Brazil • UE 34157

Joseph Diermaier • America • UE 32690

Hidan Mamudov • Balkan • UE 35574

Martin Tourish • Celtic • UE 37213

Richard Graf • Christmas • UE 32695

Penguin Polka

James Rae

Lively polka tempo ♩ = 112

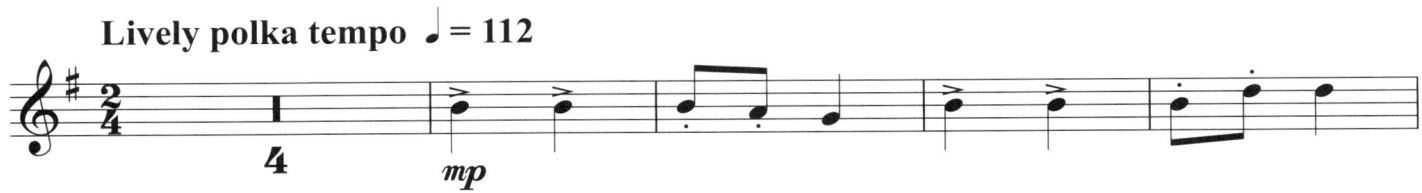

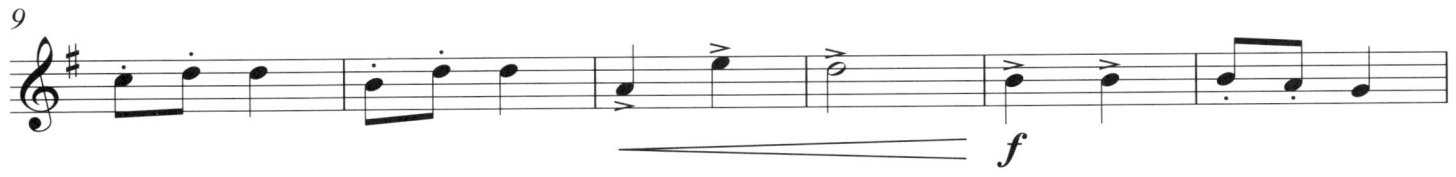

UE 21 738

Cobra Calypso

James Rae

Lively, with a bite! ♩ = 112

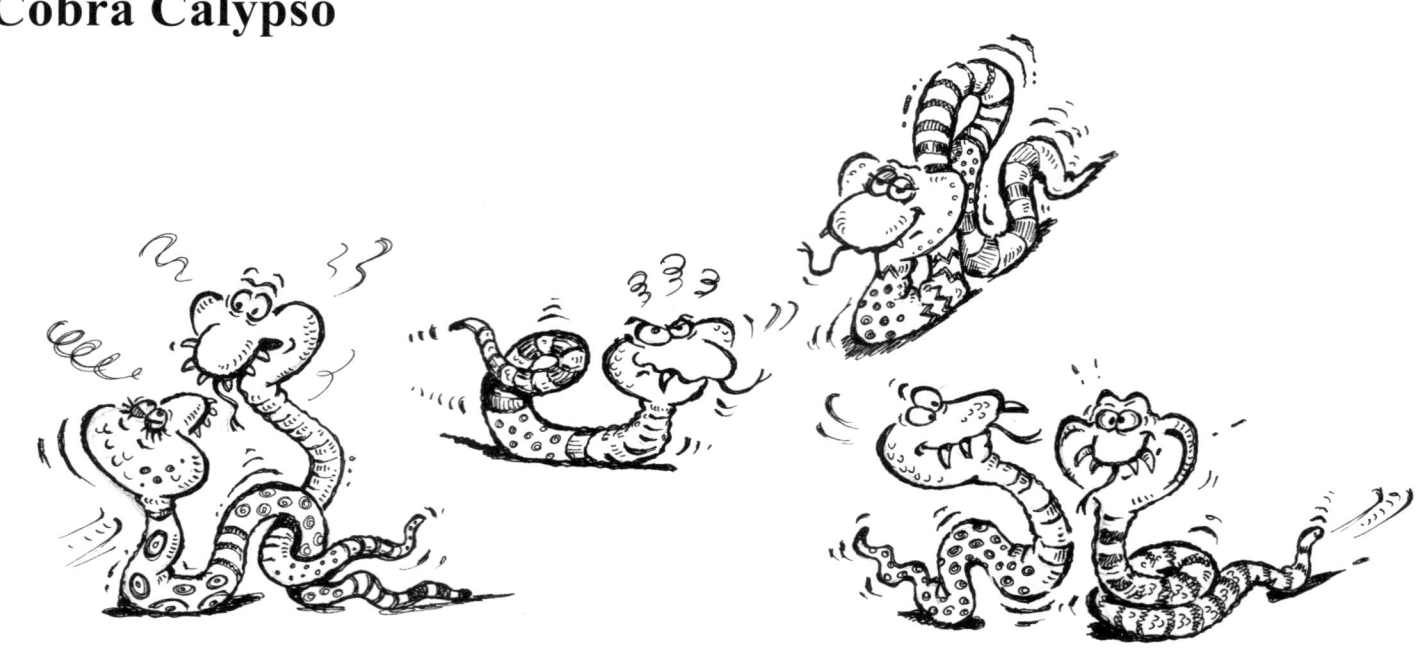

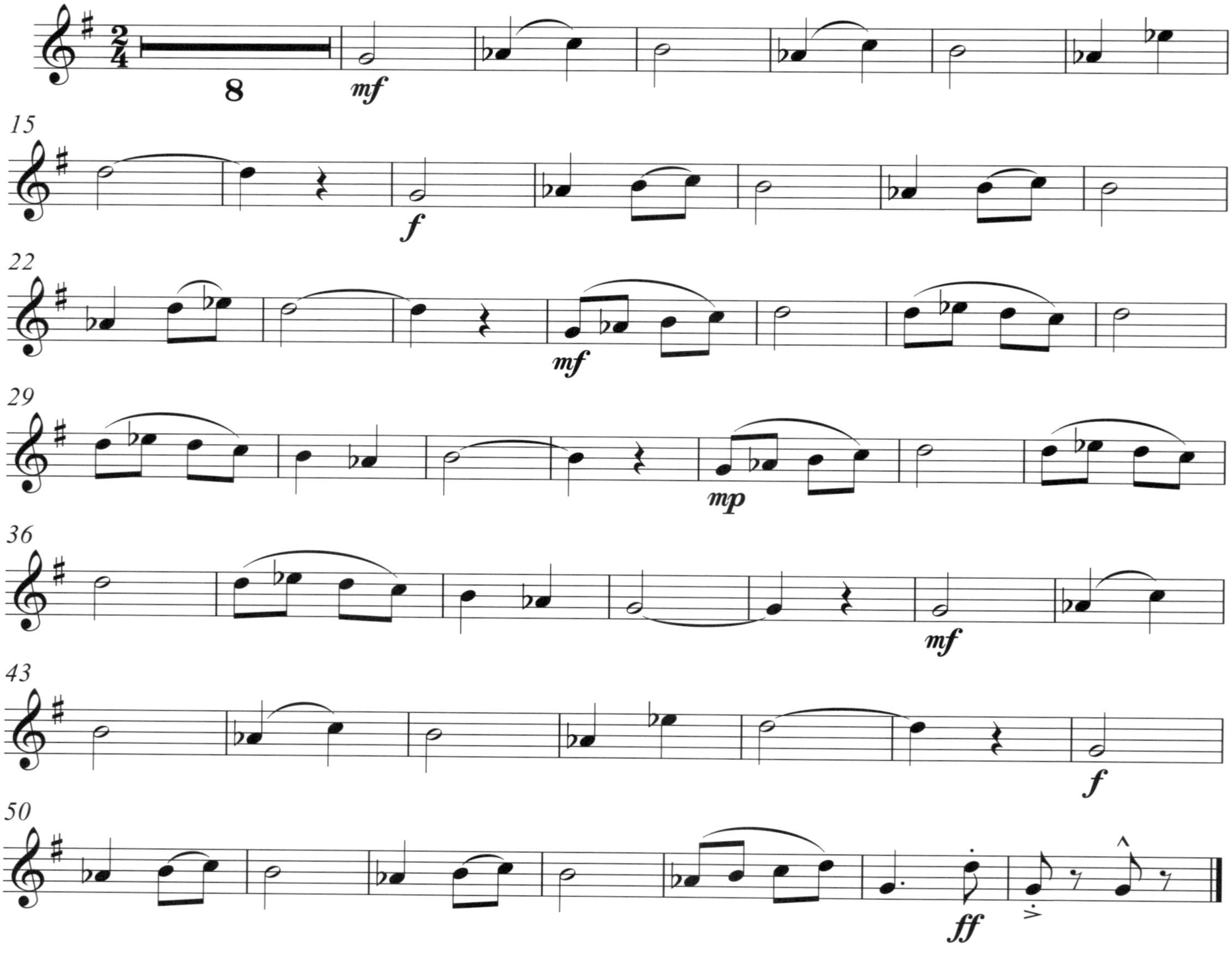

Lion Lambada

James Rae

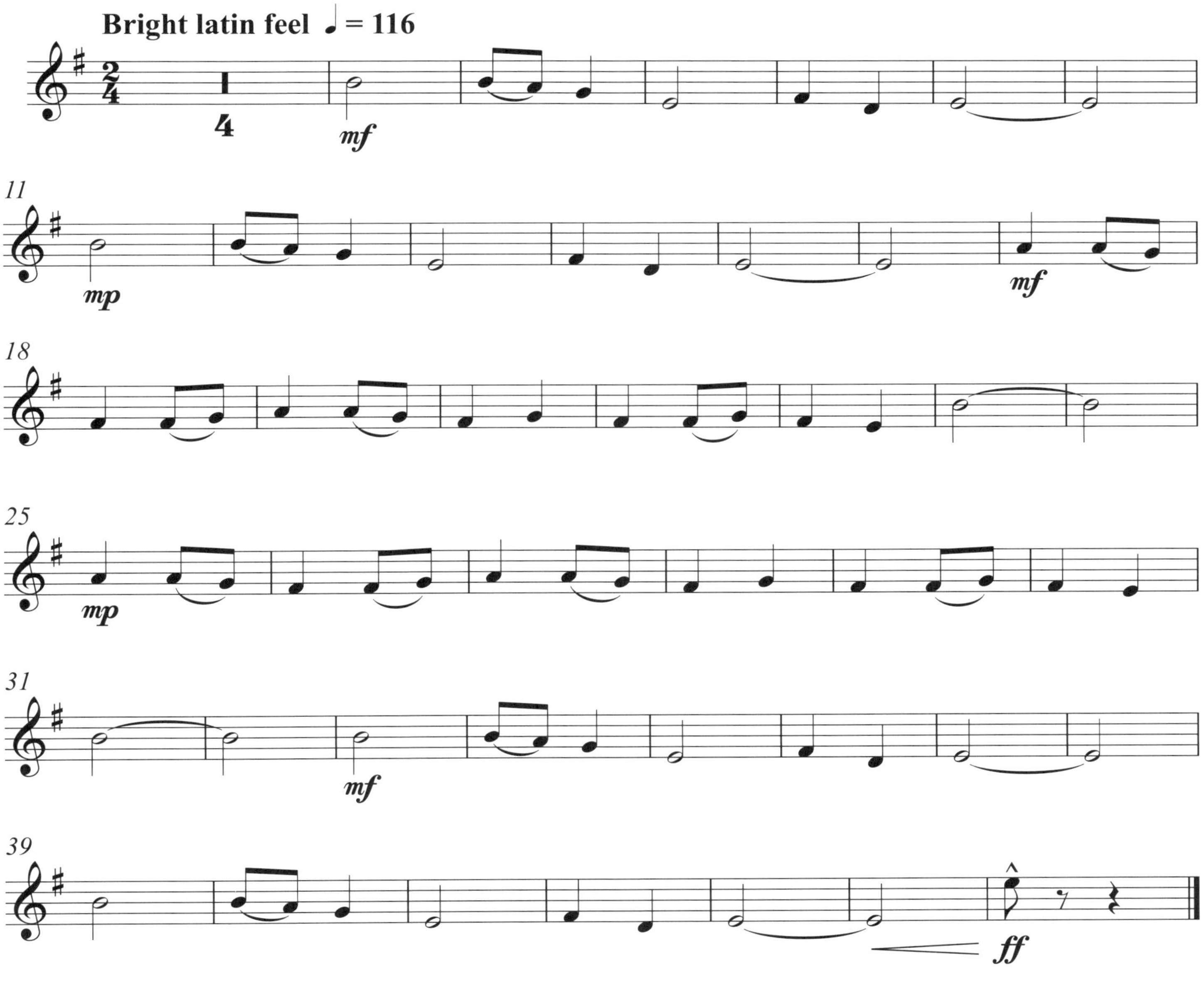

Bright latin feel ♩ = 116

UE 21 738

Chimpanzee Cha-Cha-Cha

James Rae

Hippo Hop

James Rae

UE 21 738

Giraffe Jive

James Rae

UE 21 738

Gorilla Gavotte

James Rae

Moderately menacing! ♩ = 112

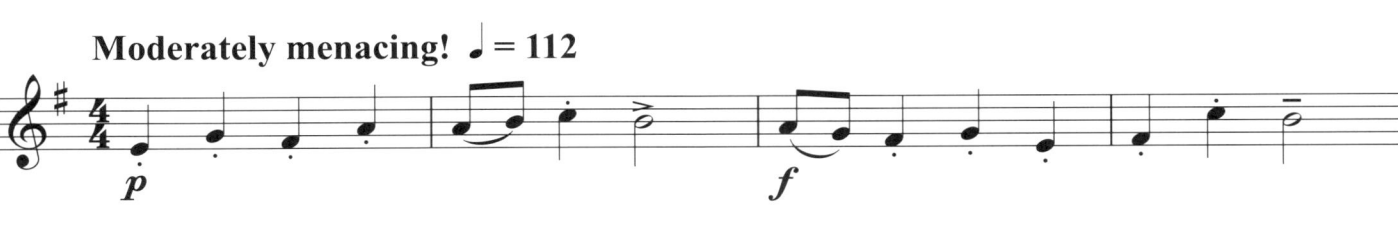

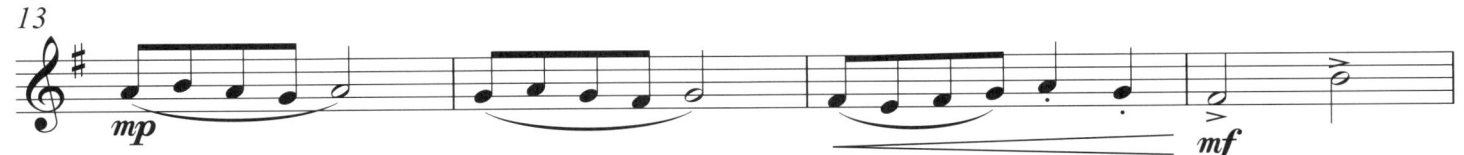

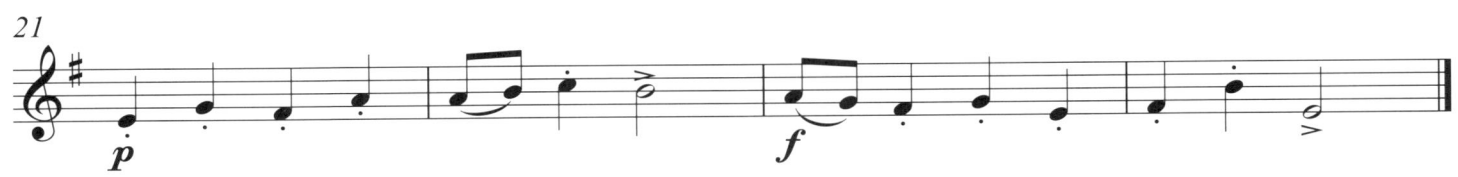

UE 21 738

Saxophone titles at an easy level

■ TUTORS

James Rae • Introducing the Saxophone (Eng.) (Alto with CD) (Beginner–3)* • UE 17 390

James Rae • James Rae's Methode für Saxophon (Germ.) (Alto with CD) (Beginner–3) • UE 31 499

James Rae • Introducing the Saxophone Plus – Further pieces complementing the tutor

(Alto and piano) • Book 1 (1–2) UE 30 420 • Book 2 (2–3) UE 30 421

Magic Saxophon (Barbara Strack-Hanisch)

Die Altsaxophonschule (Germ.) (with CD) (Beginner–3) • Band 1 UE 36 001 • Band 2 UE 36 002

Spielbuch Altsaxophon (Germ.) (Alto & piano) (Beginner–3) • Band 1 UE 36 003 • Band 2 UE 36 004

Die Tenorsaxophonschule (Germ.) (mit CD) (Beginner–3) • Band 1 UE 36 421 • Band 2 UE 36 422

Spielbuch Tenorsaxophon (Germ.) (Tenor & piano) (Beginner–3) • Band 1 UE 36 423 • Band 2 UE 36 424

■ YOUNG BEGINNERS

James Rae • Child's Play – Ein Kinderspiel • First pieces for young beginners (Alto with piano)

(Beginner) • UE 21 699

James Rae • Saxophone Debut – Solo or group learning for young beginners (Alto with piano or CD)

(Pre-1 – 1)) • UE 21 530

■ STUDIES

James Rae • Step by Step – Easy pupil-teacher studies (Beginner – 2) • UE 21 624

James Rae • 20 Modern Studies for Solo Saxophone (S / A / T) (2–7) • UE 18 820

James Rae • 36 More Modern Studies for Solo Saxophone (S / A / T / B) (1–8) • UE 21 613

Easy Classical Studies • John Harle (Ed.) (S / A / T / B) (1–8) • UE 17 770

James Rae • Styleworkout for Solo Saxophone (S / A / T) (1–5) • UE 21 232

James Rae • Jazz Scale Studies – Saxophone (S / A / T / B) (1–8) • UE 21 353

James Rae • Easy Studies in Jazz and Rock for Solo Saxophone (S / A / T / B) (1–3) • UE 19 392

■ LIGHTER STYLES

James Rae • Easy Jazzy Saxophone (A / T and piano) (1–3) • UE 16 578

James Rae • Play it Cool – Saxophone (A / T and piano or CD) (1–2) • UE 21 100

James Rae • Easy Blue Saxophone (A / T and piano) (1–3) • UE 21 262

■ ENSEMBLE

James Rae • Introducing Saxophone Duets, Trios and Quartets

Duets (1–3) UE 21 359 • Trios (1–3) UE 21 360 • Quartets (1–3) UE 21 361